THE TOP TEN
INVENTIONS
THAT CHANGED THE WORLD

Chris Oxlade

PowerKiDS press.

New York

Published in 2010 by The Rosen Publishing Group, Inc.
29 East 21st Street, New York, NY 10010

Designed and produced by
David West Books

Designer: Gary Jeffrey
Illustrator: Rob Shone
Editor: Katharine Pethick
U.S. Editor: Kara Murray

Photographic credits: 6l, Daniel Ullrich; 7t, Mark Pellegrini; 7m, eschipul: 7bl, gadl; 7br, Rama; 9t, Library of Congress; bl, N. Kent Loudon; br, Dave-F; 15m, Library of Congress; br, Rgoogin; bl, Corbis; 18l, 19t, Library of Congress; 19m, US Navy; 19b, NASA; 11l, John Kratz; 11bl, pinkiwinkitinki; 20, edkohler; 24, Incase Designs

Library of Congress Cataloging-in-Publication Data

Oxlade, Chris.
The top ten inventions that changed the world / Chris Oxlade. — 1st ed.
p. cm. — (Top ten)
Includes index.
ISBN 978-1-4358-9173-9 (library binding) — ISBN 978-1-4358-9174-6 (pbk.) —
ISBN 978-1-4358-9175-3 (6-pack)
1. Inventions—Juvenile literature. 2. Inventors—Juvenile literature. I. Title.
T48.O953 2010
609—dc22

2009018053

Printed in China

Contents

Introduction

The following inventions have been selected as the top ten from the thousands of inventions that have changed our world. It is a difficult choice to make since there are so many options to consider. So why have these ten made it on the list, and not others?

* First, the invention must have had an impact on the world within 50 years of being invented and yet must still affect our lives today.

* Second, it must be an invention, not a discovery.

The hourglass helped medieval sailors to navigate the oceans but it was replaced by the chronometer.

The X-ray, discovered in 1895, gave rise to X-ray machines, but it was not itself an invention.

✳ Third, it must be attributable to an inventor. The wheel does not make it into the top ten because no one knows who invented it.

If you disagree with the decision to include some of the inventions here, you could make a list of your own favorites.

The wheel, a hugely important invention, has no known inventor.

Hero of Alexandria invented a steam engine in the first century. Unfortunately, he did not know what to do with it and it took another 16 centuries before a usable steam engine was invented.

The Printing Press

In 1450, Johannes Gutenberg built his first printing press in Mainz, Germany. The printing press was not a new idea, but Gutenberg had invented a way of making large quantities of metal type (individual metal letters). The type was arranged to make up the words, sentences, and paragraphs on a page. Then it was placed in the press, inked and pressed onto paper. When enough copies had been printed, the type was used again to build another page. Before this, every book was copied out by hand. It allowed books to be printed in large numbers.

A piece of metal type has a backward letter on top.

THE PRINTED WORD

A copy of the Gutenberg Bible

In 1452, Gutenberg began work on his most famous work, the first printed copy of the Bible. It was finally published in 1455. He produced 180 copies, costing 30 florins each, equal to three years' wages for a clerk. But a handwritten book would have cost ten times as much. Others soon copied Gutenberg's methods, set up their own presses, and began producing books. By 1500, there were more than 200 printers in Europe, which between them had produced tens of thousands of books on a wide variety of subjects.

A modern printing press prints up to 10,000 sheets of paper an hour.

This led to a rapid spread of new ideas and knowledge that could never have happened without the printing press. Without this ability to spread information far and wide, our world might still be stuck in the dark ages.

A single page of a Gutenberg Bible was made up of about 2,600 metal letters called type. The lines of words were placed in a metal frame, positioned on the press and inked. The page was printed on damp paper, which was hung up to dry.

Today many thousands of new books are printed every week.

An electronic book, or e-book, reader displays books stored in digital form.

The Steam Train

George Stephenson (1781–1848) is thought by many to be the father of the railroad.

In 1821, the wealthy merchant Edward Pease met an engineer named George Stephenson. Pease wanted a horse-drawn train to carry coal to the town of Stockton-on-Tees, in northern England. He offered Stephenson the job of building the railway, but Stephenson convinced Pease to use steam locomotives instead of horses. Four years later, on September 27, 1825, the Stockton and Darlington Railway was opened.

At 10:00 a.m., Locomotion No. 1, driven by Stephenson, set off from Shildon, near Darlington. It was pulling 34 wagons filled with coal, flour, and more than 500 people. Some rode on top, some were in passenger wagons, and some were in a coach. At 3:45 p.m., the train arrived at Stockton. It had traveled 25 miles (40 km), with a top speed of 15 miles per hour (24 km/h).

The Skerne Bridge (right) was one of the first railroad bridges ever built. It is still in use today.

FULL STEAM AHEAD

The potential of steam power was first demonstrated in 1804, when a locomotive built by the Englishman Richard Trevithick pulled wagons at an ironworks in Wales. Early steam locomotives were slow, undependable, and often broke the iron rails they ran on. But railroad engineers, such as Stephenson, gradually improved the

In the nineteenth century, the train station became an important part of most towns.

technology, and the success of the Stockton and Darlington Railway showed that steam locomotion was the way forward. This was during the time of the Industrial Revolution in Britain, the United States, and other countries. The railroads could move huge amounts of goods

In 1869, the transcontinental railroad was completed. It connected the East Coast and West Coast of the United States.

quickly. The steam train enabled the rapid industrial growth of the nineteenth century, a revolution that changed the world forever.

In developed countries, industries depended on steam trains until the 1960s.

The Camera

Frenchman Joseph-Nicéphore Niepce was frustrated. He simply could not hold his hand steady enough to trace the image of his garden produced on his camera obscura. Niepce began searching for a way to record the image instead. Around 1816, he began to experiment with silver chloride, which darkens when exposed to light. He produced some images on paper but they quickly faded away. In 1824, Niepce tried using bitumen, a black, sticky tarlike material, which he knew turns slowly lighter when exposed to light. In 1826, he placed a pewter sheet coated with bitumen dissolved in lavender oil inside his camera obscura, pointed it out into a courtyard, and waited for eight hours. Then he rinsed away the extra bitumen to preserve the image. The result was a photograph that still exists today.

The camera obscura was a popular drawing aid in the 1700s.

FROM SNAPSHOTS TO MOVIES

In 1829, Niepce joined forces with another Frenchman, Louis-Jacques Daguerre, and continued to experiment. In 1837, four years after Niepce died, Daguerre perfected the daguerreotype, a photographic process using silver iodide coated metal sheets. A new process using negative images recorded on glass plates came into use 20 years later. Heavy equipment and dangerous chemicals meant photography was only for the experts. But in 1889, American George Eastman began selling a lightweight camera with a roll of celluloid film in it. The same film was used in the first movie cameras, which took images, one quickly following another, along the roll. This was a giant step on the road to the modern movie business, making the camera an invention that has opened up the world to us all.

A young Abraham Lincoln captured by daguerreotype in 1846

The Eastman Kodak Brownie of 1900 was light, easy to use, and cost $1.

In 1895, the Lumière brothers in France were the first to show movies to a paying audience.

Modern camcorders and cameras record images digitally.

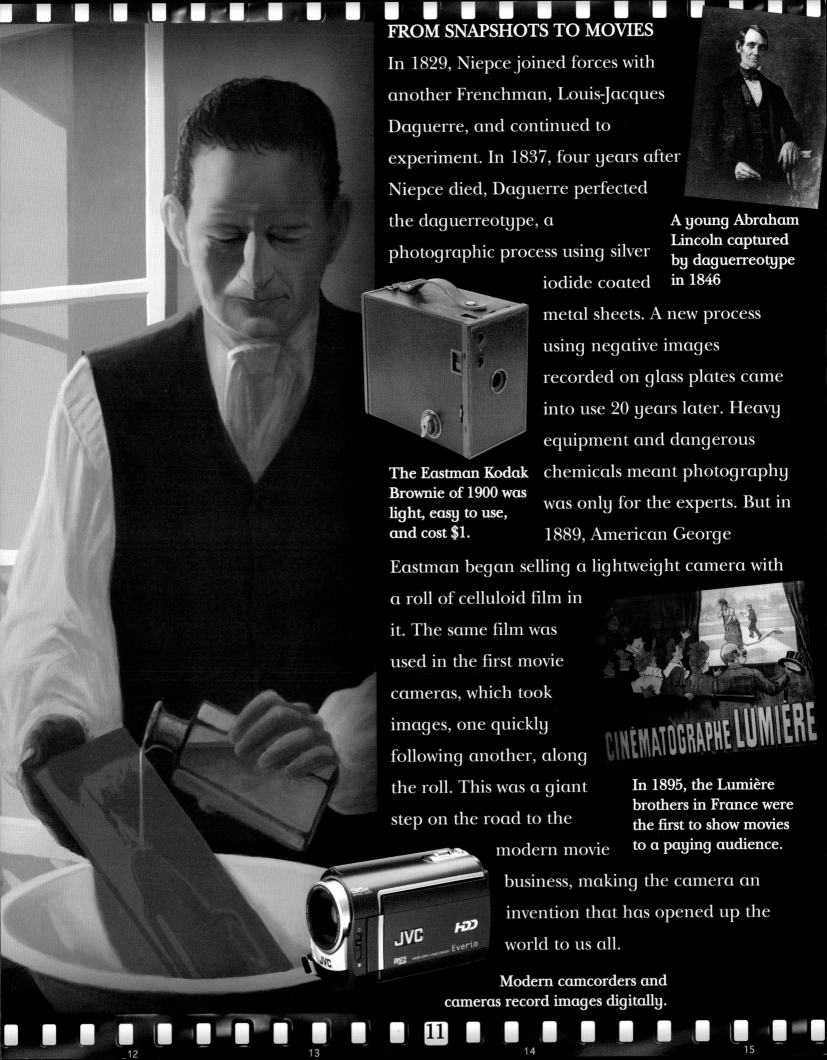

The Telephone

"Come here, I want to see you!" called Alexander Graham Bell. They were ordinary words, but extraordinary in this case because they were the first ever to be uttered over the telephone. It was March 10, 1876. Bell was in his workshop in Boston, Massachusetts, speaking to his assistant Thomas Watson. Bell had been trying to find a way to send several telegraph messages along the same wire at the same time when the idea of sending speech along a wire came to him. He made transmitters to change sound into an electrical signal and a receiver to turn the signal back into sound. Bell filed a patent for his telephone just hours before rival inventor Elisha Gray did.

Early telephones had separate earpieces and mouthpieces.

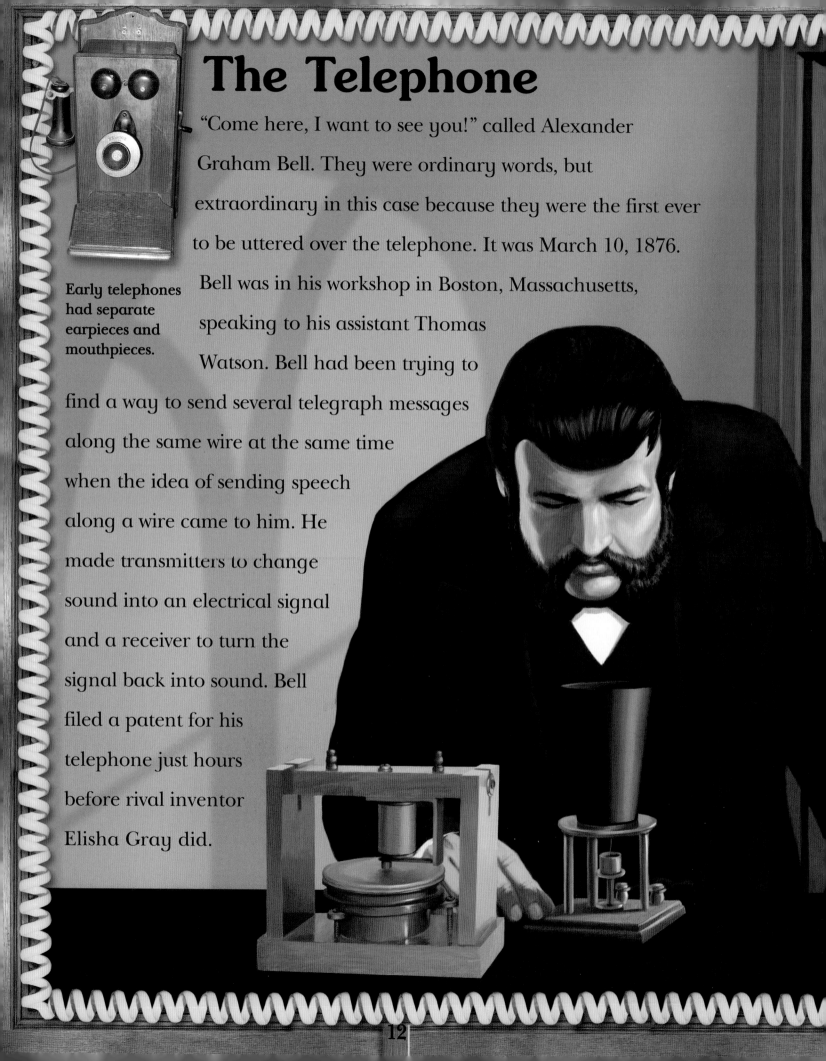

IT'S GOOD TO TALK

Until the invention of the telephone, the only way to get a message to somebody far away quickly was the telegraph. The sender had to visit a telegraph office to send the message and at the other end the message had to be delivered. The new telephone was useless, though, without networks to link receivers together. These were built quickly, though, locally at first and then nationally and internationally. Less than ten years after that famous first call, there were 150,000 telephone subscribers in the United States alone. As early as the 1890s, automatic exchanges opened, allowing people to call each other without talking to an operator. Bell's invention was where the technology that allows us to talk and send messages instantly to people anywhere in the world got its start. This communication system has dramatically changed the way we live.

A telegraph key used to tap out Morse code

A telephone exchange around 1900

A 1930s dial telephone

Cell phones such as the iPhone also act as music players, cameras, and game players.

13

The Independent

Henry Ford, Miracle Maker
INDEPENDENT CORPORATION
May 1, 1920   10 Cents

Henry Ford (1863–1947) was the founder of the Ford Motor Company. He built his first car, the Quadricycle, in 1896.

The Car

Henry Ford did not invent the motor car. That honor went to German engineer Karl Benz, who built the first car in 1886. But Ford made the car popular by building cars made for ordinary people. Ford's success came from just one car, the Model T, which was unveiled at the Ford Motor Company's Detroit factory on October 1, 1908. It was different from other cars of the time in that it was easy to drive and easy to maintain and repair because of interchangeable parts. It was also a lot cheaper because over the next few years Ford developed mass

production. The Model T was pieced together on an assembly line, as most modern cars are. Each worker added one or two parts as the car passed by on a conveyor belt. It was an efficient system that kept costs low and production high.

Robots do much of the work on modern car production lines.

MOVING THE MASSES

At first, Ford's Model Ts were built one by one by hand, in the same way as other cars. This method was slow and made cars expensive, and only the rich could afford them. In 1908, Ford's workers made just 11 cars in a month. But in 1914, when Ford's assembly line was up and running, a Model T rolled onto the road every 3 minutes. That year, Ford built more cars than all the other U.S. car manufacturers combined. As efficiency improved, the Model T became cheaper and the cars were bought by a public excited about having their own vehicle. By 1925, half the cars in the world were Model Ts. When production stopped in 1927, more than 15 million had been built.

By then, car technology had moved on and it has continued to move on ever since. Today the car is a key part of the global economy.

Karl Benz's Motorwagen was the first vehicle with a gasoline-powered engine.

In 1900, fewer than 1,000 cars were made in the United States. In 1940, that figure had risen to 4.5 million.

Too many cars cause congestion and pollution.

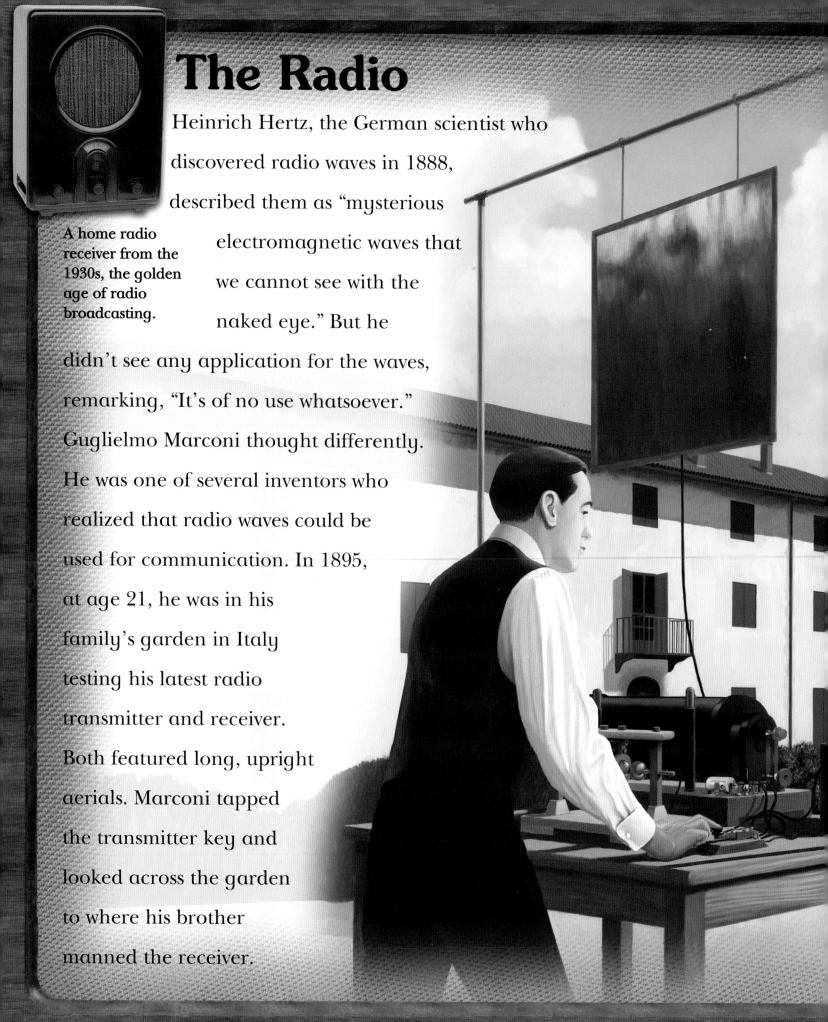

The Radio

Heinrich Hertz, the German scientist who discovered radio waves in 1888, described them as "mysterious electromagnetic waves that we cannot see with the naked eye." But he didn't see any application for the waves, remarking, "It's of no use whatsoever." Guglielmo Marconi thought differently. He was one of several inventors who realized that radio waves could be used for communication. In 1895, at age 21, he was in his family's garden in Italy testing his latest radio transmitter and receiver. Both featured long, upright aerials. Marconi tapped the transmitter key and looked across the garden to where his brother manned the receiver.

A home radio receiver from the 1930s, the golden age of radio broadcasting.

Marconi's brother immediately waved his handkerchief that day. The receiver had detected the radio signal. Later Marconi sent his brother to a hill 1 mile (2 km) away. His brother fired a gun to signal that the radio waves had arrived. The age of radio communications would soon follow.

This is America..

... where you can listen to your radio in your living room — not in a hideout. Where you are free to hear both sides of a question and form your own opinion ★ This is <u>your</u> America

... Keep it Free !

WIRELESS PROGRESS

At first radio was used to send electric telegraph signals. This was called wireless telegraphy. One of its first applications was ship-to-shore communications. Soon after the *Titanic* sank, every large ship was required by law to have a wireless operator listening for Morse code messages 24 hours a day. By 1906, amplitude modulation had been invented, which allowed sound to be sent by radio. The first radio stations went on air in 1919, and by the end of the 1920s radio broadcasting was widespread. Radio waves were also used for the first television broadcasts. Today, radio has a bewildering range of applications. The invention of radio has led to many wireless tools that we use every day, including baby monitors, global positioning systems (GPS), cell phones, and wireless computer networks.

The sinking *Titanic* used Marconi equipment to send one of the first wireless distress signals.

This is a World War II propaganda poster. In wartime the radio kept civilians informed.

The 1954 Regency TR-1 was the world's first pocket radio.

This 50-foot (15 m) radar dish is used by NASA to track spacecraft.

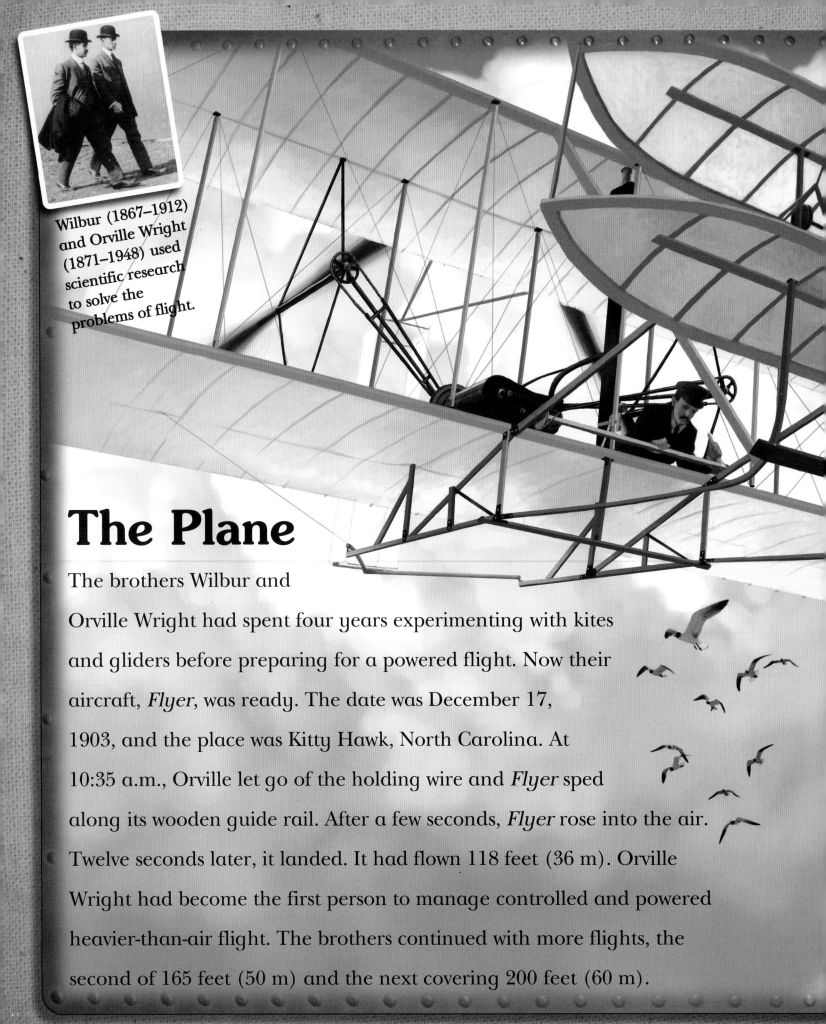

Wilbur (1867–1912) and Orville Wright (1871–1948) used scientific research to solve the problems of flight.

The Plane

The brothers Wilbur and Orville Wright had spent four years experimenting with kites and gliders before preparing for a powered flight. Now their aircraft, *Flyer*, was ready. The date was December 17, 1903, and the place was Kitty Hawk, North Carolina. At 10:35 a.m., Orville let go of the holding wire and *Flyer* sped along its wooden guide rail. After a few seconds, *Flyer* rose into the air. Twelve seconds later, it landed. It had flown 118 feet (36 m). Orville Wright had become the first person to manage controlled and powered heavier-than-air flight. The brothers continued with more flights, the second of 165 feet (50 m) and the next covering 200 feet (60 m).

PLANE POWER

In the years after the Wright brothers' famous flight, other pioneers built and flew their own aircraft. But ten years later, aircraft were still oddities. The outbreak of World War I in 1914 changed that.

A World War I recruitment poster

Otto Lilienthal (1848–1896) was an early pioneer of flight. He flew in homemade gliders.

Military leaders quickly realized that the airplane would be a useful tool for spying on and attacking the enemy. Aircraft technology quickly improved as each side tried to build better aircraft than the other.

After the war, bombers were converted into the first airliners and the first airlines began operating. For those who could afford to pay, journey times were reduced from days to hours. By the 1930s, planes were carrying passengers around the globe. The speed and size of aircraft increased quickly again during World War II (1939–1945). The war saw the invention of the jet engine, which powers today's sophisticated airliners. From a short hop just over 100 years ago to worldwide air travel today, flight has changed the world.

Flying boats, such as this Catalina, were used by air forces, navies and airlines.

At around noon, Wilbur began a fourth flight. He covered 850 feet (260 m) in 59 seconds. Later, a strong wind picked up the plane and rolled it over, smashing it beyond repair.

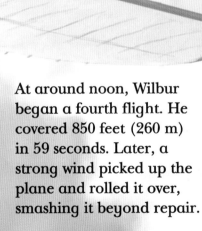

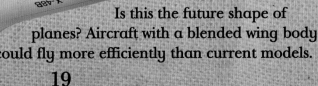

Is this the future shape of planes? Aircraft with a blended wing body could fly more efficiently than current models.

The Television

Television requires a device that detects the amount of light coming from each part of a scene. This information is sent using electricity to another device that displays the image. This process is repeated many times a second to make the image move. Scottish inventor John Logie Baird gave the first demonstration of television in 1926. To the shock of the invited audience, a flashing, blurred picture of his assistant's face was shown in the next room. His "televisor" included large spinning disks full of holes to scan the scene and rebuild the picture.

A modern high-definition flat-screen television

Baird's first system produced poor quality images made up of just 30 vertical lines, with 12 pictures a second, but later he built an improved 240-line system.

Television viewing in 1928

An early TV remote

New from Japan–the TV that thinks it's a phone

EVOLUTION OF THE TUBE

While Baird was creating his television system with its mechanical disks, other pioneers were working on completely different electronic systems. These used a device called the cathode ray tube to capture and display moving images. American inventor Philo T. Farnsworth is thought to have given the first demonstration of an electronic television system in 1927. Early television broadcasts, which began in 1928 in some countries, were sent by both mechanical and electronic systems. But by the mid-1930s, the superior picture quality of electronic systems killed off mechanical systems, such as Baird's. The new gadget proved very popular as prices fell during the 1950s. In the early 1960s, television overtook movies as the world's most popular form of mass entertainment. Since then, the world has remained hooked on the most popular device ever invented.

A receiver from 1946

Color television arrived in the 1950s.

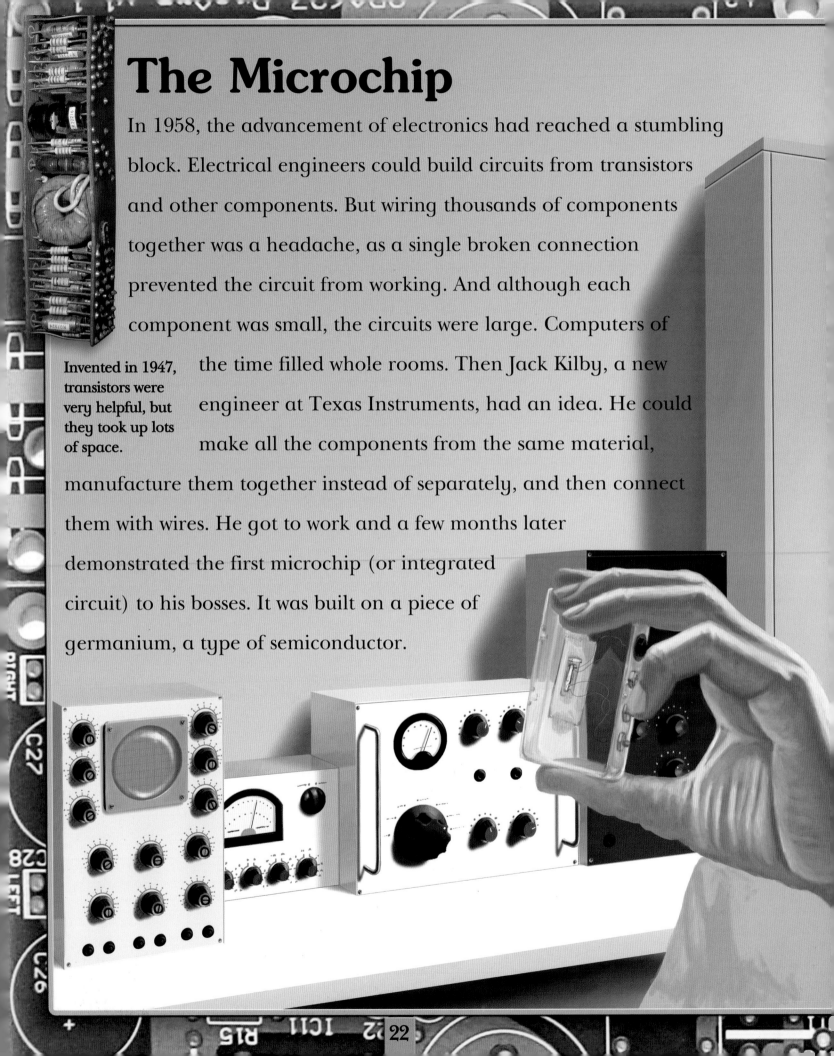

The Microchip

In 1958, the advancement of electronics had reached a stumbling block. Electrical engineers could build circuits from transistors and other components. But wiring thousands of components together was a headache, as a single broken connection prevented the circuit from working. And although each component was small, the circuits were large. Computers of the time filled whole rooms. Then Jack Kilby, a new engineer at Texas Instruments, had an idea. He could make all the components from the same material, manufacture them together instead of separately, and then connect them with wires. He got to work and a few months later demonstrated the first microchip (or integrated circuit) to his bosses. It was built on a piece of germanium, a type of semiconductor.

Invented in 1947, transistors were very helpful, but they took up lots of space.

The invention of the microchip was a huge leap forward. It made miniaturization of electronic circuits possible. Jack Kilby went on to coinvent the personal calculator, the first consumer product to popularize the new technology.

SMALLER, FASTER, CHEAPER

Kilby was not the only scientist working on integrated circuits. Six months after Kilby's demonstration, Robert Noyce, working at Fairchild Semiconductor, built a microchip from silicon. This was the ancestor of all modern microchips. Microchips were first used by the military, but within a few years appeared in consumer devices such as televisions and radios, making them cheaper, smaller, and more reliable. Today there are microchips in almost every electronic device, from car keys to supercomputers. Our modern lifestyles, with cell phones, the Internet, and video games would be impossible without them. The global digital revolution created by the microchip is here to stay.

Modern-day chips are very complex and increasingly tiny.

Microchips made the U.S. space program of the 1960s possible.

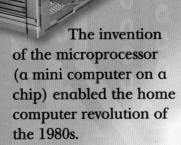

The invention of the microprocessor (a mini computer on a chip) enabled the home computer revolution of the 1980s.

Microchips have made machines from spacecraft to electric toothbrushes more efficient and reliable, as well as safer.

23

The Web

In 1980, English software consultant Tim Berners-Lee was working at CERN, the European Particle Physics Laboratory in Switzerland. While there, he wrote a program for storing and linking files on his computer. He called the

Web pages offer information instantly, at the press of a mouse button.

program "Enquire," after a Victorian encyclopedia he read as a child. In 1989, Berners-Lee took "Enquire" and extended it to link the files on one computer to files on any other computer on a network. He wrote a coding system called HTML, which let people put links in their files, created software for accessing the files across the Internet, as well as a program called a browser to display the HTML files. This collection of linked information was dubbed the World Wide Web. It was launched in 1991.

User-created Web pages like Wikipedia maintain the spirit of Berners-Lee's original vision for the World Wide Web.

GETTING CONNECTED

The World Wide Web could not work without the Internet. The history of the Internet dates back to 1969, when the U.S. government's Advanced Research Projects Agency (ARPA) linked two computers at different laboratories in California so that they could share information. Other computers were quickly added, forming a network called ARPANET. The Internet was born in the mid-1970s when various other networks around the world were linked to ARPANET. It allowed computer users around the world to share information and send e-mails. Since Berners-Lee invented the Web, Internet use has ballooned. In 2008, there were more than a trillion Web pages, including on-line encyclopedias, stores, instant news sources, and social networking sites. The Web has revolutionized the way information is shared, making the world a smaller place than ever.

The original computer mouse from 1967. Its inventor, Doug Engelbart, was also the first person to connect to ARPANET.

The Web is run by server farms, which are computers that store and distribute information on the Web.

Wireless networking allows people to use the Web from almost anywhere.

25

The Best of the Rest

THE ELECTRIC MOTOR AND DYNAMO

The first electric motor was demonstrated by the British scientist Michael Faraday in 1821. He showed that electric current flowing through a magnetic field produces movement. A decade later, Faraday showed the opposite effect. Moving a magnet inside a coil of wire produced electricity in the wire. In 1832, France's Hyppolyte Pixii put Faraday's findings to practical use by building the first electricity generator. Today, most of the electricity we use is produced in power stations by generators. Electric motors drive machines from power drills and clothes driers to robots and hard drives.

Faraday at work in his laboratory.

THE WHEEL

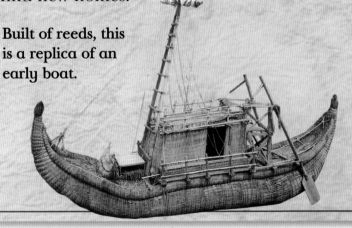

Wheels are not just for vehicles. Nearly every modern machine uses wheels in some way. Even computers use wheels inside their hard drives and DVD drives.

The wheel is one of the most important inventions of all time. We don't know exactly how or when the wheel was invented, but ancient engravings from Mesopotamia (part of modern-day Iraq), dating back to 3500 BC, show that the potter's wheel and simple wheeled carts were already in use.

THE BOAT

The first boat was probably simply a hollowed-out tree trunk or a raft of logs. We don't know when people started traveling on water, but it must have been tens of thousands of years ago. Whenever it happened, the boat allowed people to travel long distances to hunt, trade, and find new homes.

Built of reeds, this is a replica of an early boat.

Today, giant metal ships carry vast amounts of raw materials, such as oil and grain, and finished goods, such as cars and toys, across the globe. The modern world economy would be impossible without them.

TIMEPIECES

Harrison's marine chronometer

In ancient times, people tried many different ways to measure the passing of time. Their inventions included water clocks, sundials, sand timers, and burning candles. Mechanical clocks were hopelessly inaccurate until 1656 when Dutchman Christiaan Huygens invented the pendulum clock, whose speed was regulated by a swinging pendulum. One place where an accurate clock was necessary was at sea, where knowing the exact time was needed to calculate longitude. Navigation was improved when, in 1759, English clockmaker John Harrison built a marine chronometer that was accurate to 30 seconds in a year. Accurate electronic timekeeping is common today. Almost every electronic machine has a built-in clock, either for its own use or for our information.

GUNPOWDER AND GUNS

Gunpowder was invented in China around AD 950, but it was another 300 years before the Chinese used it to fire their newly-invented cannons. Gradually the technology spread to the rest of the world. In the sixteenth century, ships were armed with cannons and handheld guns were being used in battle, although they were unreliable and slow to reload. By the nineteenth century, the musket and field artillery gun were causing heavy casualties in war. At the battle of Waterloo in 1815, 45,000 men (one-third of those fighting) were killed or wounded. Later in the century, the machine gun was invented by American Richard Gatling. It was used to devastating effect during World War I. Most famous of modern guns is the AK-47 assault rifle, designed by Mikhail Kalashnikov in 1947. It is the weapon of choice for revolutionaries, private armies, and terrorists all over the world.

An AK-47

MONEY

When people first traded, they bartered with each other, perhaps exchanging milk for some eggs or crops for clothes. A commodity later came to be used to represent the value of things. This allowed buying and selling using money to take place. The Aztecs, for example, used cocoa beans. In Mesopotamia (in modern-day Iraq), around 3000 BC, a shekel was a measure of grain that was used as money. In Britain, a pound was originally a pound of silver. The first coins were pieces of gold or silver that had value. Banknotes were first used in China in the seventh century.

Lydian coins from 640 BC

PAPER

The earliest recorded forms of paper, made from the papyrus plant, were used in Egypt around 3500 BC. True paper is believed to have originated in China around the second century, although there is proof that it was used even before this time.

Chinese woodblock print from 1249, Song Dynasty

The use of paper spread from China through the Islamic world, and it was first produced in Europe in the early twelfth century. In the early nineteenth century, mechanized paper production meant information in letters, books, and newspapers could be exchanged cheaply, spreading knowledge worldwide.

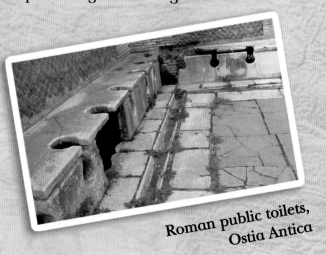

Roman public toilets, Ostia Antica

TOILETS AND SEWERS

The first toilets were built around 2350 BC in a palace in Mesopotamia (in modern-day Iraq). Underneath the simple pedestal was a sewage pipe. The ancient Egyptians and Romans also had toilets but only for the privileged. The first flushing toilet was created in 1596 by Englishman Sir John Harrington. It was not until the nineteenth century, though, that towns and cities had sewers and toilets available for all. Even today, nearly 40 percent of the world's population still does not have access to one.

Pont du Gard, Roman aqueduct

AQUEDUCTS

An aqueduct is a channel, often supported on piers, that carries water from one place to another. The ancient Romans are famous for the aqueducts that carried water to drinking-water fountains in their cities. The ancient Egyptians and people of the Indus valley, though, had built aqueducts for irrigating their crops thousands of years before.

MEDICAL SCANNERS

In the early 1900s, the Italian radiologist Alessandro Vallebona proposed using X-rays to produce an image that went all the way through a person. This is known as tomography. The first tomography machine was the PET scanner. The PET (positron

The first commercial CT head scanner. *Inset*: Scan of a skull.

emission tomography) scanner of 1958 was used especially for taking images of the brain. This was followed by the CAT (computerized axial tomography) scanner and the MRI (magnetic resonance imaging) scanner.

The *Glasses Apostle* by Conrad von Soest (1403)

LENSES

The earliest evidence of lenses comes from the ancient Greek writer Aristophanes, who wrote about a "burning-glass" (a convex lens used to focus the Sun's rays to produce fire). Early lenses were also used as magnifying glasses. Accurate lenses made telescopes and microscopes possible. These inventions led to many scientific discoveries. Most importantly, lenses correct sight defects.

REFRIGERATOR/FREEZER

Refrigerators and freezers allow the long-term storage of food both at home and in the food-supply chain. Domestic electric refrigerators became widely available in the 1920s. Before then, outdoor ice houses were used for cold storage.

An early refrigerator

Timeline of Inventions

		Invention	Influence
ANCIENT	4000 BC	SAILBOAT Egypt	Makes trade possible by sea.
	3500 BC	PAPYRUS Egypt	Allows writing of records with ink.
		THE WHEEL Mesopotamia	Allows heavy loads to be moved easily.
	3000 BC	MONEY Mesopotamia	Allows buying and selling of goods.
		AQUEDUCT Indus Valley and India	Helps irrigate crops to increase yields.
MEDIEVAL	AD 950	GUNPOWDER China	Makes firearms possible.
	1000	SPINNING WHEEL India	Important for advancement of textiles.
	1450	**THE PRINTING PRESS Johannes Gutenberg, Germany**	**Begins the rapid spread of information.**
MODERN ERA	1596	FLUSH TOILET Sir John Harrington, UK	Reduces smells but only for the rich.
	1608	TELESCOPE Hans Lippershey, Holland	Leads to the discovery of planets and moons.
	1656	PENDULUM CLOCK Christiaan Huygens, Netherlands	Allows for accurate timekeeping.
	1712	**THE STEAM ENGINE Thomas Newcomen, UK**	**Brings power whenever it is needed.**
	1826	THE CAMERA Joseph-Nicéphore Niepce, France	Allows events and views to be recorded in pictures.
	1876	THE TELEPHONE Alexander Graham Bell, United States	Allows people to talk over long distances.
	1886	**THE CAR Karl Benz, Germany**	**The start of the automobile revolution.**
	1895	THE RADIO Guglielmo Marconi, Italy	Allows wireless signals to be sent over long distances.
20TH CENTURY	1903	**THE PLANE Wright Brothers, United States**	**Powered flight becomes a reality.**
	1926	**THE TELEVISION John Logie Baird, UK**	**The birth of the television industry.**
	1945	ATOMIC BOMB Manhattan Project team, United States	Reveals the power of atomic weapons.
	1958	**THE MICROCHIP Jack Kilby, United States**	**Miniaturized electronic devices become possible.**
	1975	PERSONAL COMPUTER, Steve Wozniak, United States	Brings computing to the masses.
	1977	CELL PHONE, Bell Labs, United States	Allows phones not on fixed lines to be used.
	1991	**THE WEB Tim Berners-Lee, Switzerland**	**The start of the Internet revolution.**

Glossary

World Events

Settlement of first towns and cities.

The ancient Egyptian civilization begins.

World's population reaches 14 million.

Viking Leif Eriksson sails to North America.

The Hundred Years' War between France and England ends.

William Shakespeare is writing plays.

The world's population has grown to more than 500 million.

Europeans are settling in the Americas.

Beginning of the Industrial Revolution in Europe.

Chocolate is invented.

Mark Twain writes *The Adventures of Tom Sawyer*.

The Statue of Liberty is unveiled.

The first modern Olympic games were held (1896).

End of World War II.

Rock and roll music shakes the West.

Jaws is the first modern blockbuster movie.

The first Star Wars movie is released.

World's population is more than 5 billion.

camera obscura (KAM-ruh ub-SKYUR-uh) A box with a hole or lens in one side that produces an image on the other side.

electromagnetic waves (ih-lek-troh-mag-NEH-tik WAYVZ) A form of energy that travels in waves of electricity and magnetism.

information (in-fer-MAY-shun) Knowledge or facts.

networks (NET-wurks) Collections of computers connected to each other to share information.

paragraphs (PAR-uh-grafs) Groups of sentences about certain subjects or ideas.

pendulum (PEN-juh-lum) A rod or string with a weight at the bottom that swings from side to side.

receiver (rih-SEE-ver) A device that detects radio waves.

semiconductor (seh-mee-kun-DUK-tur) A material that can act as both an electrical conductor and insulator.

signal (SIG-nul) An electric current or radio wave that changes strength or shape to represent information.

telegraph (TEH-lih-graf) A communications system that used simple on and off signals to represent letters and words.

transistors (tran-ZIS-turz) Electronic devices that work like switches.

transmitters (trants-MIH-terz) Devices that send out radio waves.

Index

Web Sites

Due to the changing nature of Internet links, PowerKids Press has developed an online list of Web sites related to the subject of this book. This site is updated regularly. Please use this link to access the list:
www.powerkidslinks.com/topt/invent/